The Green Flamingo

By David Pedemonte-Forte

Copyright © 2014 All rights reserved.
No part of this book may be reproduced or copied in any form without the written permission of David Pedemonte-Forte. All rights reserved.

The Green Flamingo by David Pedemonte-Forte
Copyright © 2018 by David Pedemonte-Forte
All Rights Reserved.
ISBN: 978-1-59755-492-3

Published by: ADVANTAGE BOOKS™
                www.advbookstore.com

This book and parts thereof may not be reproduced in any form, stored in a retrieval system or transmitted in any form by any means (electronic, mechanical, photocopy, recording or otherwise) without prior written permission of the author, except as provided by United States of America copyright law.

Illustrations by David Pedemonte-Forte

First Printing: October 2018
18 19 20 21 22 23 24 25   10 9 8 7 6 5 4 3 2 1
Printed in the United States of America

Everglades. The big storm was coming. It was hurricane season in Florida and all of the animals were looking for shelter.

There was a large village of Flamingos.
All the females started gathering their eggs
as they are starting to head towards higher grounds.
But the storm was heading quickly towards their
direction so the Flamingos had to move quickly.

While all of them were flying away from their nests to safety… one Mama Flamingo left her egg behind.

They got away just in time before the hurricane had arrived at their spot. Meanwhile, the storm was so devastatingly large, it destroyed houses, crops and farms.

A farmer had a large barn where he kept all of his chemicals he uses for his plants. It was very close to where all the Flamingos had their nests.

The force of the storm was so strong, it rocked the barrels back and forth, causing them to fall over, and causing a big spill which drained down…

...onto the egg... the same egg that Mama Flamingo had unknowingly left behind. The egg was sitting in that chemical for a long time.

Days later, the storm had finally ended and the sun was gleaming upon the egg. It started cracking apart slowly and a Baby Flamingo broke out. It was a girl.

By the time all of the Flamingos started coming back to the village, Mama Flamingo frantically flew to her nest in desperation of finding her egg that she left behind.

And, much to her surprise, Mama Flamingo found her newborn baby Flamingo, but was born... different. She was born... green.

Upon seeing her for the first time, Mama Flamingo ran away, frightened at the sight of her young one that was born... green.

One day, a female Flamingo was right there by the Baby Flamingo's side. She brought food and fed her. She took care of her until one day she could fly. That female Flamingo... was her Mama.

Several months later, The Green Flamingo has grown up. Mama Flamingo went back to their nest to feed her young Flamingo and, to her surprise, she was not there.

The Green Flamingo was in shock with what she saw a few feet from where she was.

There were a large gathering of Alligators.

Fortunately, the Alligators could not see her because not only did the chemicals change her color that blends well with the bushes and leaves, it also changed her scent because though the Alligators could smell Flamingos, they could not smell HER. She knew that she could not move anywhere from this spot, otherwise they would see her.

"Gather around... Tonight's meeting will begin," said The Alligator King. "The hurricane drew all of the animals out of the everglades. They all moved to higher grounds and we have stayed without food."

"But I have discovered that not too far from here, there is a Flamingo village where there are thousands of them. We can have enough food for all of us. I want us to rest up for the night and when dawn is coming, which will be very soon... we feast."

As dawn was coming, The Green Flamingo waited patiently until the alligators moved away. She then flew rapidly to her village and warned her family of what she had overheard and for everyone to evacuate.

As the light of the early morning arrived, The Green Flamingo and her family already flew away, when hundreds of Alligators marched in their now empty village. The Alligator King was so furious, his followers were so scared to even look at him.

With her mother by her side, the Flamingos apologized for making fun of her and finally accepted her as their own, no matter what her color is. They were all safe and sound, and it is all thanks to...

The Green Flamingo.

The End

I have created this book for a purpose; for everyone to remember that we all have certain inabilities... We are not to discriminate against each other because we don't want to be discriminated against. We are not to bully each other because we don't want to be bullied. No matter what ethnic background, color, size or disability...
we are all born in this world for a purpose.

- DAVID PEDEMONTE-FORTE

www.ingramcontent.com/pod-product-compliance
Lightning Source LLC
LaVergne TN
LVHW081400060426
835510LV00016B/1925